HOW TO FIND, PITCH AND WIN YOUR FIRST WEB DESIGN CLIENT

Matthew Higgins

Matthew Higgins

Get the Sample Proposal Download Pack:
http://bit.ly/findpitchwinsample

Thanks to Chris Spooner (spoongraphics.co.uk) for the social
network icons used

ISBN: 987-1-4467-2388-3

Getting Ready

Identifying Your First Client

Next Steps

Bidding

Afterword

6

Getting Ready

Starting out as a freelance web designer is no mean feat!

Around the world, hundreds of 'script kiddies' who have taught themselves HTML are turning to the web every single day, looking to make quick, easy money with as little effort as possible.

With so many new, developing and experienced designers out there, it can be difficult for any individual, whether new or experienced, to stand out above the rest, and this can mean that when bidding on a project, even the most talented designer will be brushed aside if they don't get noticed, and don't get themselves seen.

Over the next few pages, I will take you through the process of identifying potential clients (that's the '**Find**' part), writing a kick-ass proposal to make them fall for your services instantly (the '**Pitch**'), and how to reply to them when they tell you their verdict (hopefully, this is the '**Win**' part).

Even if you are unlucky, there are things you can do to leave it nice and open for them to come back if their chosen designer lets them down)

8
Personal Branding

There are much more in-depth sources of information on personal branding available, whole books dedicated to it, and I am only going to give you a brief overview of what you need to do.

If you're looking to go into business as a freelancer, there's a good chance you're already pretty good at marketing yourself, as most entrepreneurial types are, and this is all you need.

There are two faces to maintaining a strong brand when you're working as a freelance web designer; first, you need a unique selling point, second, you need a consistent visual identity that flows through your documents, and your website.

The Unique Selling Point

Every single article, blog and book about branding will talk about knowing and understanding your unique selling point, and being able to apply it to every piece of communication you use. The easiest way to apply this is to decide what makes you different from all of your competitors, then come up with a few derivatives, and end up with a list of eight or so key words, which get reused again and again.

This means that when you write a blog post, or start writing your first proposal (that bit comes later in the process), or even a single, 140 character tweet, you need to be thinking about how it links in with your unique selling point, and how people will learn to associate it with you.

The truth is that most web designers don't think they need this, however, when you have hundreds of pages of material that supports a single image of you, it will end up rubbing off on your next potential client.

10

The Visual Identity

The second element is your visual identity. Big businesses typically spend unbelievable amounts of money every year refining their logo, colour palette, typography and print and web designs, and while this, almost always, gets results, it's not really worth spending any money on when you're just starting out.

If you're friendly with a graphic designer, a logo will make you stand out immediately, however, some very simple logos can be very effective.

The key is consistency, and once you find something that works for you, like a colour scheme, some lesser known free fonts and a particular style of page layout, you're onto a winner, as long as you never let a document leave that doesn't match!

Create some templates that match and you will appear to take so much care with every document you prepare for your clients that they will never cease to be impressed, boosting their impressions of you instantly.

Do you need a logo? Logos are thought of as being cold and corporate, they put distance between you and your client. When you are working as a freelancer, this is not what you really want.

There are things you can do. A lot of freelancers keep some elements of a visual identity, however the 'logo' element is typically their name in a distinctive font or style, or a soft friendly image that becomes associated with them, without becoming a hard-edged cold logo.

12
Personal Website

Taking on board everything listed about creating and developing your own brand, it's essential that these are consistent throughout your personal website. You need to create something that engages the potential client, as in many cases, the website will be the first thing of your's that they see.

If you have one, keep an up-to-date portfolio online, and make sure that your site is the absolute best it can be, even if it means getting a little help.

> If you really feel the need to get someone in to create your website, do not have a link back to them on your homepage. Even if you're a developer, it does not look good to say 'Here's someone I recommend', when you want people to be considering you for work.

If you have a blog, it's worth updating it regularly, and keeping in mind your unique selling point and it's derivatives as you do. Again, there are whole books dedicated to business and personal blogging out there. Keep on topic, keep encouraging comments and keep it up to date.

If you can't afford the time to keep it up to date, you're better off scrapping it than keeping lots of old articles, or take a look at services like Tumblr, which allow you to maintain a blog that's typically shorter and simpler than a traditional blog.

If you promote yourself well on the social networking sites, it's a good idea to give some links to your profiles from your personal website, hopefully someone visiting will find their way back to your Facebook page and 'like' you, or 'follow' you on Twitter, instantly highlighting you to all of their friends, which can only be a good thing.

Identifying Your First Client

This section covers what a lot of people find very hard, actually coming across someone who you can sell to.

With so many options out there, you can certainly make a good job of it, and while you may well be pushed aside with a lack of experience, you can always keep trying!

16
Building Your Portfolio

Most potential clients will look very closely at examples of your work, and depending on how big a project it is, may also contact people you've done work for in the past. If you don't have a large portfolio of previous work, there are a few simple things you can do;

Make sure you have a brilliant website of your own to promote yourself as a freelancer. Make sure it looks and works flawlessly, and that there are no silly mistakes, like typos, or claiming it is valid HTML, then it actually turning out not to be.

Do a little free work, and put this in your portfolio. We will look at this in a bit more detail later on, but the best bet is to find a charity local to you, and 'donate' them a free website as a gift in kind. You can even soak up a little publicity for this, which might even generate you some more leads later.

Real World Networking

Lots of work is generated through word of mouth, so it pays to have an existing network of people, and make it known to them that you are going into web design. Once enough people know, it will just slip out somewhere along the line, and eventually, someone, somewhere who is in need of a website will hear about you.

Absolutely always carry a few business cards, and when you're around new people, even in a social setting, always be ready to 'switch' into business mode if you identify someone as a prospective client.

It's also good to generally get yourself out and about when you're looking for work. There are a few ways to get yourself a few more contacts, although, some can be a little tedious. It's never bad to get yourself out and about and mixing with your potential clients, although it can be a struggle to not come across like a salesperson who is only interested in generating leads.

I met a client in a sandwich shop once. It was lunchtime and it was very busy, he had a big table to himself, the last in the room. I asked if he'd mind me sitting at the table, I commented on the brand name on his folder and before long, we got chatting. I'd mentioned in passing that I was a freelance designer, and as he was leaving, I passed him a business card, and suggested he give me a call if he wants help with anything. The next time I heard from him, he was looking for a website.

18

This can work in any situation, a good place to generate lots of interest are the open 'Start your own business' seminars that are run by educational establishments and local governments for aspiring entrepreneurs.

While you may not be quite ready to put yourself forward to be involved or a speaker, if you are around the nearest restaurant or cafeteria at lunchtime, you can instantly generate lots of connections who are; looking to start a business, don't have a website for their business yet and are keen to network themselves. It's a win-win situation.

When you're meeting new people, all the usual rules about personal presentation apply; dress smartly, but not too smartly, be polite, smiling and punctual. If you're not sure about this, the best place to look is dating advice websites! What you do to impress a hot date is exactly what would leave prospective clients with a brilliant impression of you!

Online Networking

Every day, hundreds of millions of people use social networking sites to connect with the people around them, the businesses they use and the places they visit.

While people will rarely log into Facebook with the intention of looking for a web designer, it can be brilliant in terms of publicity if you regularly pop up in the news feed, and before too long, someone will look and think, "Well, one of my friends has used this guy", and see how highly recommended you come!

Without this, the chance of you being recommended is significantly smaller.

20

Facebook

Facebook is the most used social networking website available, and it is If you post "I do websites, message me for one" as your Facebook status, most people will probably laugh at you! If, on the other hand you enter it into your Bio and work info, then, occasionally post the odd status update about web design, or a link to the last site  you worked on, people **will** start to click through and find you.

In case you forgot to mention, all of your Facebook friends will see that you're working as a freelance designer, and most people are happier having someone they know do their work for them.

If you have any previous clients, do become friends on Facebook. Amongst other things, it lets you keep track of their birthday, and a personal birthday card (a real physical card, not a "happy birthday" wall post) to each previous client will keep you fresh in their mind if they ever need anything in the future.

Make sure your privacy settings let people you don't know see your work info and bio, and message you! In 'Privacy Settings' use the 'View As' tool to see what they can see.

LinkedIn

LinkedIn is another good social network, and if you already have a good network of business contacts on LinkedIn, it's well worth referencing your skills in your profile, however it's generally not the best source of leads, since it is very restrictive, and prospective clients don't get to see very much about you unless they are 'Introduced' by  a mutual contact. It would work, but it's rare to get any business that way.

It's good practice to, every time someone hands you their business card, have a quick look for them on LinkedIn and add them to your professional network. It allows you to build your network, and making sure this gets done in a timely manner will make sure they are fresh in your mind when you do. This has the advantage of increasing your chance to get a 'recommendation' from them while you are still fresh in their mind.

22

Twitter

If you use Twitter, it can be brilliant for getting noticed, and boosting your existing reputation. You can tweet virtually anything, and it's very short and instant, meaning it's much less commitment and effort than a blog. You need to be very careful not to annoy your followers, because at a certain point, any follower will be very quick to 'Unfollow' you after a certain amount of annoyance.

Retweet interesting things, make some comments relating to web design and, to a lesser extent, everyday life, and get some links on there. Make sure you remember to fill in your bio and link back to your own website too.

DeviantArt

If you are a designer, rather than a developer, a brilliant, but often forgotten site to try would be DeviantArt. While lots of site members are traditional artists, there is a community of web designers uploading their work and giving each other critique and feedback, and it's not uncommon for knowledgable developers to skim through the work of candidates when looking for a designer to collaborate with on a project.

DeviantArt has it's own culture and takes a bit of getting used to, however it is a very good way to connect with other designers, and to share work and feedback.

24
Freelance Network Websites

There are lots and lots of websites where you, as a freelancer, can build your own Facebook-style profile, and prospective clients can come along and list the jobs they need doing, and you, along with tens, if not hundreds of other designers can submit Proposals or Bids to do the work.

It can be unbelievably difficult to differentiate yourself from the competition on these sites, however there are a number of strategies that you can employ;

- Seem interested, ask questions and attempt a meaningful discussion with the prospective client. Most of these sites let you ask 'prebid' questions, and these are a great way to be able to tailor your bid even more, especially where the question and answer are given privately.

- Personalise every bid, and make the potential client feel like you have put a lot of time and effort into their bid. If you give a fairly typical, copy and pasted statement from every other bid you submitted, it often seems like you actually don't care.

- Start Work without winning. You can get all of your ideas together, and product a little of the project for the potential client straight away. Especially if you don't yet have a proven track record, this can be very good to show that you are capable. On the other hand, you may waste a lot of time, and the work may go to someone else. The best idea is to do a little work on something that is useful on a lot of projects, or that you can sell afterwards, so that if you don't win, you haven't really lost anything.

There are some techniques employed which don't have quite the same success, or that may seem like a good idea at the time, but are actually quite detrimental in the long term

- Undercut all of the other bidders. This is not really recommended, and rarely works, if you do bid a stupidly low amount and win, you will end up making a loss when your time is taken into account. It also makes you look desperate, and like your work may not be up to scratch.

- Write a very long proposal. While a good, detailed proposal is good (that's in the next section), it needs to be very concise. Hit the key notes and avoid waffling. Most of these sites allow you to write a short, written piece, then, optionally, extend it slightly with an attachment. An introductory piece of around 80 characters with an attached PDF of your proposal (the one you create in the next section) is by far the best bet.

The problem with these websites is that they are often expensive to use. You will receive a certain number of 'bids' for free each month, then, more will cost you. The best thing to do is to put a lot of time and effort into each, and you may be lucky enough to not need any more.

While the prospective client is in the process of deciding, make absolutely certain that you respond to everything very promptly, positively, and politely. Make sure everything they associate with you is brilliant!

26
Freelancer Forums and Job Boards

Lots of websites include forums and job boards for freelancers. These can be a great way to find potential clients who are specifically looking for work.

Most of the same rules apply as do for the specific Freelance network websites, however you have a bit more flexibility. On a lot of these websites, especially the forums, everything is public. This means it's a bad idea to post your proposal and quotation, or to ask any compromising questions which might give the game away to your competitors.

Always opt to phone, e-mail or private message potential clients rather than having a discussion publicly. Where this isn't an option, post a reply giving your e-mail address or phone number, and ask them to contact you directly. This is also very good, as there's a chance that someone else looking might come direct to you rather then posting their own job on the site.

Free Work

There are several schools of thought regarding doing free work, and 'mates rates'.

The blogs of lots of web designers have tackled this issue, and the strong, consistent theme throughout all of them is simply "Don't".

There are however some times when doing a little free work can do you the world of good for your own development, especially when you don't have much of a portfolio to begin with. It is never a good idea to work for free for a client who would be able to pay, which covers most businesses, however for small, local charities, clubs and voluntary groups, a gift-in-kind can go a long way.

There are, however, a few significant dangers with doing any work for free;

- You may end up doing a lot more work than you expected. This is why it is essential that you write a contract, explaining what you are doing free, and what is not covered. This simply means that your 'client' can't turn around and try to demand anything extra, and if they do, and it's not in the contract, you don't need to 'argue' with them to reach a resolution.

- It may take up too much of your time. If you agree to, it is well worth building in a significant amount of contingency. When you give your estimate of how long the work will take, multiply it by at least three. This ensures that if anything additional comes up, you don't end up delivering the free work late.

28

As mentioned, you absolutely need a contract. Set out what you will do, and that you won't charge them to do the work listed on the contract, but anything further will be charged. It is up to them whether they agree or not.

You should make sure that you don't take on any free work that will take up too much time, this will cause you more problems. You should aim to take on small, simple, 'first website' projects.

There is also some potential to sell add-ons and development for this project, even, potentially with a 'Charity discount' or similar. 'Donating' a free first project can do you a lot of good in the long term, however you need to be absolutely positively careful not to bite off more than you can proverbially chew.

Next Steps

There's a very small part in between finding your client and being ready to pitch to them.

There are two main questions you need to ask;

The first you ask your client, and that is "**What do you want?**", and the second you ask yourself, which is "**Do I want to take this on?**".

30
Making Contact

Depending how you identified the potential client, there are several things you can do next. Your aims needs to be;

To quickly obtain enough information to produce a brilliant proposal

The best bet is a phone call, however an e-mail will work too. The information you need to get out of the potential customer is;

- As much detail about their own requirements as they can give you. This isn't too critical, but it will allow you to be even more accurate and specific when you write your proposal.

- Do they have their own budget? They don't have to tell you, but it will give you an idea of whether you are both expecting the same amount of work from the project.

- When do they want/need it completed by? This is simple. If it's absolutely necessary within a certain time, and you know you'll be too busy or it's not long enough, tell them that! They will be more impressed with your honesty, and may well consider you for any future work.

Make sure that when you talk to them, you have a pen and a notebook handy, it would be very embarrassing, and harm your professional reputation to guess details that you don't know, or to get something wrong directly to your client, after they told you!

Making Your Decision

Now, it's your decision time.

Can you do this?

You need to be certain that this job is one you want to do, and that you know how to do it, before you take on something you can't do, and end up looking a complete fool!

Take as long as you need to be sure of this, but remember that you need to respond to your client and 'Wow' them with your proposal, so don't take so long that you've found someone else.

I've never taken too long on this. On little, simple projects, it's an instant 'Yep', however for some projects, it might be a good idea to sleep on it, or have the weekend to yourself to decide.

If you don't think you can, it's best to tell the client this. You can be as straight and 'frank' with them as you like, however avoid placing any blame on them. If you go to your client and say "That's far too much work for anyone to do in four days", you are effectively telling them that their expectations are too high, and while this may well be true, you're best not sounding like you think it's their fault.

If you say that "Personally, I would need at least eight days to complete the work to a high standard", you are making it seem as though by giving you the job, and a little extra time, they will get a brilliant job.

32

They will either come back to you and lower their requirements slightly, or they won't budge on the needs, but your reputation hasn't harmed by a half-baked job, and as ever, they are free to get back to you should they choose to, either if their chosen designer lets them down, or if they have another job for you to do in the future.

If you're completely satisfied that doing this job isn't going to result in any harm to your reputation, then it's time to leap ahead and crack on with your proposal.

Bidding

There are lots of ways you can 'bid' on a project, and the way you do so will inevitably come down to the choice of the potential client.

Some ask for you to visit them and give a presentation, others ask for a less formal, face-to-face meeting, but the vast majority are happy with a string of e-mails and some time on the phone.

34
The Proposal

Whichever method you go for, presenting a written proposal will give the potential client something to look at, something to think about, and something to 'remember you by' and, frankly, most others don't bother, and it enables you to really stand out above the crowd.

If this is your first project, you are probably bidding on a project that has been advertised through one of the freelance network websites, or doing some work for a business or personal contact. Regardless of which method you are following, you still should send a written proposal.

The best bet is to attach it to an e-mail as a medium to high quality PDF file. Good enough that if it was printed with a good quality office printer, it would still maintain the 'brilliance' that the document needs. Depending on the nature of the project, and the budget, it may also be worth printing a high quality copy onto brilliant white paper and posting it. Every little improvement you make, like choosing brilliant white presentation paper, or high quality recycled paper (remember to point this out in the document) over economy copier paper, makes you seem like a genuine hard worker, with your own high standards.

Get started with your choice of design or word processing package. Pages, from Apple's iWork suite, is by far my favourite, although I've used Microsoft Word and Adobe InDesign successfully before. It depends on what you're comfortable with, and how much emphasis you want on the looks, and how much on the content. This is where having a strong visual identity comes into it's own. If your new written proposals match your portfolio, Twitter profile, business cards and anything else, you're slowly strengthening your identity as a designer in the minds of your potential customers.

Depending on personal choice, you can decide exactly how you proceed in terms of design and layout. While I've seen some laid out like magazines, which does look very good, the majority are set out like a typical word processing document. This includes lines of black text on a white background, the occasional chart or table and good, strong, consistent styles throughout the document.

There are a few personal choices, for example, do you base the whole document on a series of A4 sheets, which are easier to print, or do you go for a different layout, like an A5 booklet. This is solely down to personal choice, but be aware that occasionally clients may ask for a hard copy if you're e-mailing it, so try to design something that you could print if you had to.

36

Front Cover

The front cover is completely down to you, however it's good practice to include a 'To:' and 'From:' near the top, these can appear just like on a memo, and could be written as 'Prepared For:' and 'Prepared By:' or similar.

One option is to go for a high quality design, for example, a photographic background with a slogan on or similar, or a large, interesting diagram. It's a case of, as when designing anything, creating an attractive design where you entice the user to read on a little further.

The other option is to just include the title and your branding. Think of this as the 'minimalist' approach. It allows the document to be clearly identified and explains what it is really clearly. Where you go for this option, it's best to aim for a title, exactly in the middle of the page, of 'Website Proposal', and then the name of the project or company.

It's also a good idea to include, along the bottom of the page or similar, your contact details and a link to your portfolio or blog.

Contents

You don't need a contents page. Depending on the size and nature of the job, you may or may not want to include one. Where each section covers less than one page, it is simply a waste of space including one.

If your sections are longer, then you may like to include a contents page. It makes the document more user-friendly, especially if you or the recipient decides to print it.

Depending on how well formatted your document is, and how much faith you have in the software you're using, you may use the built in 'automatic table of contents' function that most word processing software, and desktop publishing packages include.

Assuming you will be sending a PDF of the file, either by itself or with a hard copy, it's well worth making the table of contents link to the respective pages of the document. It's easy enough to add links to a document, and most software preserves them when you convert it to PDF.

Introductions

The first main section needs to be pretty typical between any proposals that you write. You need to introduce yourself, your company, anyone else you will be working with, and the facilities you have available.

These sections often end up sounding a little like a job application. You need to sell why you are ideally suited to the job, and to make yourself sound well-rounded and interesting. Someone your prospective client wants to work with.

For me, the first paragraph is usually about me personally, and I include things like;

- My skills – I include an overview of the skills I offer, and where a more obscure skill is needed for a specific project, I often expand on this, listing some details of previous jobs I worked on using them.

- Other Interesting Things – I also include some details of me, and what I do outside of the web design. There's no desperate need for this, however it does allow me to present a more rounded image, and it has the potential to make a good conversation starter for further discussions with the prospective client.

- My Team – When I work with other people, for example, I have a graphic designer I usually work with; it's worth including some information about them. This may be provided by them, or abridged from their own website or professional profile.

- Facilities – I list the various tools and facilities that I have available, some specifications of my workspace, the software I've got, the professional networks I belong to, and the tools I use to manage, coordinate and keep track of my work. This gives clients a little additional peace of mind, showing that I've got backing me up.

- Previous Work –At this point, it's a good idea to give some examples of notable or high profile projects you've worked on. It can give you a bit of an edge if you've got something substantial that you can squeeze in early on, however including this at this point is far from essential.

40

The Brief

You now need to explain either the brief that you've been given, or the problem that you are looking to solve;

If you've been given a creative brief for a new project, it's a good idea to either quote the whole lot here, or to quote small sections, along with some information about how you would go about fulfilling it. It's important that if something is unclear, you make an effort to understand the requirements fully; otherwise you end up looking stupid if you have described something completely irrelevant.

If the scope of your work is to 'Improve an existing site', this is where you need to work through and review the existing site, along with what could be improved on every front. Make an effort to take little things into account, like accessibility and functionality.

If you've been brought in to work on a small, specific task, this would be a good time to list what you need to do with it, break it down, and identify what you could do that would ensure every element of it works correctly.

Eventually, you end up with a mixture of quotes of the potential customer and your views on how to do the work. Depending on the exact nature of the task, you may need to present this as a situation analysis, and a list of project targets that will solve the perceived problem.

Stating your project goals early on allows you to focus on and link back to these throughout the remainder of the proposal. This gives you some consistency and makes everything appear very neat and focused.

Your Solution

The remainder of the document is dedicated to you presenting exactly what you would do to solve the perceived problem or meet the criteria of the given brief.

The first thing you need to do is give a brief, written outline of what you would do for the client. Two sentences or less, to simply identify what the main things you can do are. You should describe exactly what you would end up with.

You then need to break it down a bit further, listing little things, like what software you would use, and what the user would need to do, for example, regarding updates to the content, and what you have done to allow it to be expended in the future.

By thinking about future updates now, you are opening yourself up to the possibility of updates in the future coming back to you, especially if they were your idea to being with!

42

Scheduling

It's a good idea to give the potential client an idea of how long it will take, and to divide everything into neat phases. I usually break the project into a small number of main phases, usually less than 10. Under each of these I give a description, and an approximate duration (for my projects, these are usually between three and ten days), with a little 'contingency' built in, usually by multiplying my estimate of the duration by two.

Doubling it ensures that clients aren't disappointed if the work is just slightly behind "schedule", however are usually pleased if their work is completed ahead of time.

Providing a table that shows what each phase involves, how you will achieve it and how long it will take it always a good idea, and the potential clients absolutely love it! They can see exactly how long everything is going to take, and can keep track of it perfectly as you get along, as providing there is enough contingency built into your estimates, the prospective clients will love the way that you meet every single one of them ahead of time!

Budgeting

The first important point to understand is the difference between a 'Quotation' and an 'Estimate'.

When writing a proposal, I always give an estimate, which is usually a page of the proposal. Generally, it will be formatted and organised similarly to an invoice, however will include some notes under each item in the list, and will give an approximate cost of the total project, typically including;

My time to complete the project; a little more on calculating this in a moment.

- Hosting for the project; personally, I have a large reseller account that I use, which means I get a little extra control over everything. This isn't compulsory, and some clients prefer not to have it hosted by me. That's ok too. I generally look for the most appropriate package from another host, then reduce the price slightly. I'm still able to make a small, ongoing profit, and the client gets to feel like they are making a saving compared to the same package from another host.

- Advertising; I usually 'sell' some advertising on the side of all projects, usually only a tiny amount, and I set up Google and Facebook to deliver a few highly targeted advetisments. This is good, because I can then monitor the impact for myself, and use this later to demonstrate to the client how powerful the medium is, and encourage them to let me buy them some more (with a tiny commission, keeping them close with an ongoing commitment is the real benefit)

- Any 'Premium' services that get bought in; I never try to market these, but small, additional services, like specific pieces of software, or anything that needs buying in. If the customer has asked for it, they won't be too upset if they are expected to pay for it separately to the rest of their package.

- Any other workers who do specific tasks; this could be developers, custom plugin authors, or visual identity specialists, anyone who gets brought in to do a specialised job should have been asked to provide either a quotation or an estimate, and which it is needs to be provided to the client, which immediately shifts blame away from you if the specialist's terms change unexpectedly later.

It's essential that you calculate your own hourly rate and that you calculate it pretty well, otherwise it will cause it's own barrage of problems later.

You need to take a lot of things into account, although the most important, and you should know this already, is whether you want this to be your primary source of income.

If you do, then it's relatively simple; you take your 'salary' amount, whatever you feel suits you, add any costs that are purely for your business, and divide by the number of billable hours you have each year.

If you are doing this part time, it's less straightforward, however the same principle applies; start with an amount of income you think you can realistically generate (be a little conservative for your first few months, until you find your feet), plus any costs that are purely for business, and divide by the number of hours you spend working.

Since many designers publish their own hourly rates, it might be a good idea to investigate how much higher or lower than theirs yours is, to give you an idea of how sensible your rates are.

46

The Cover Letter

This page is often forgotten, or replaced by a two line e-mail message, which the proposal gets attached to. It's essential that you get the covering letter spot on, because it will be either the first or last thing that the prospective client looks at.

Firstly, make sure you've got at least a basic letterhead, matching the branding of the rest of your material. While it makes sense to have a stock letterhead that you re-use, be very careful that you don't get into a habit of using a standard cover letter. Write every single letter for each proposal you complete.

You need to think about the following;

- Thank them for allowing you to submit your proposal, it's just basic courtesy.

- For the purpose of being polite and professional, thank the prospective client for helping you with the proposal, whether they met with you, provided information by e-mail or took part in a meeting with you by telephone.

- Explain that the attached or enclosed proposal had been prepared personally based on their situation and requirements.

- Briefly outline the next steps. If you didn't provide a quotation, you may need to, or you may require a certain amount as a deposit before work is completed. Certainly point out that is is standard practice for a contract to be signed before you start work.

- Offer to answer any questions that the potential client may have. This makes you seem more interested and personal.

The best bet is to provide this letter as a PDF, either appended to the front of the proposal or as a separate file when you e-mail the proposal, or, if you send a written copy, send a printed copy.

Afterword

I've been as careful as I can not to be overly prescriptive. While I've included a sample, it's hardly something you can copy/paste into your next proposal.

Brilliant customer service as a freelancer is about being individual, and about clients enjoying working with you. There are lots of ways you can do this!

I hope that armed with this basic guide, you will be able to find your first client, write a top-notch proposal, and successfully please your first paying customer.

Have a look online at some blogs, discussions and articles, particularly in web design and development communities about how to please your clients, and keep an eye out for anything you notice which you can stow away for the future.

Overall, while it may well just be your way of paying the bills, try and enjoy what you're doing, because when your happy and comfortable with your work, your clients will be happy!

Happy clients = more clients.

More clients = more money!